Samsung Gala:

The Complete User Mani
Professional Cinematic Vide____ ____ ___ ____ography Tips and
Tricks Using Samsung Galaxy S21, S21 Plus & Ultra

Curtis
Campbell

Disclaimer

The information in this book is based on personal experience and anecdotal evidence. Although the author has made every attempt to achieve an accuracy of the information gathered in this book, they make no representation or warranties concerning the accuracy or completeness of the contents of this book. Your circumstances may not be suited to some illustrations in this book.

The author disclaims any liability arising directly or indirectly from the use of this book. Readers are encouraged to seek Medical. Accounting, legal, or professional help when required.

This guide is for informational purposes only, and the author does not accept any responsibilities for any liabilities resulting from the use of this information. While every attempt has been made to verify the information provided here, the author cannot assume any responsibility for errors, inaccuracies or omission.

Printed in the United States of America

Table of Contents

INTRODUCTION

The Samsung S21 has a front facing camera just like the other models; the front camera is located at the middle top area of the Samsung S21 device, just right below the speaker. A little space to the left is where the proximity sensor is located, although it cannot be seen physically. The image below shows the complete description of what we're trying to explain above. You can also see the volume increase and decrease keys at the side of the device which can be used to take photos instead of tapping the shutter button. Also, the volume keys can also be used to take screenshots or perform a screen record when held together with the power button. The front facing camera is mainly used for taking selfies and video calling purposes.

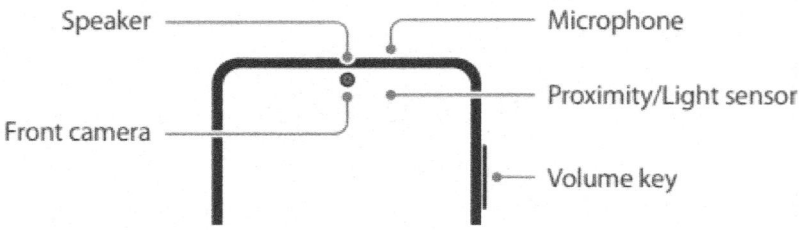

Now let talk about the rear cameras, the Samsung S21 model has three rear cameras accompanied with a single flash light. The rear cameras are arranged horizontally on top of each other with a barrier making it look specific. The flash light is located just outside the barrier and right beneath it is a microphone. The rear cameras are of three different types of cameras called; the ultra-lens, Ultra-wide lens and the telephoto lens, each having a different megapixel. Capturing crisp and HD photos, you'd need to make use of the rear cameras, also for capturing wide areas such as valleys, mountains or skyscrapers, the ultra-wide camera will do the job perfectly.

This guide contains everything you need to know about the Samsung S21 cameras, start your journey as a professional photographer as you read this amazing guide.

CHAPTER ONE

How to quickly open the Camera app

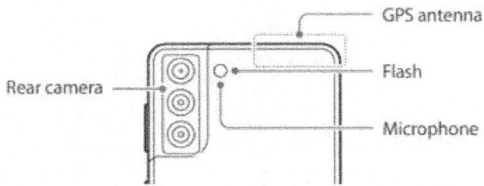

How do you get to the camera application on your Samsung S21 device? It's pretty easy and normally you should be able to do it. The camera application is one of the mostly used pre-installed application on any device, although this is depending on the user, but, seven out of ten people uses the camera application often more than other apps, which is why the camera app is usually located in the lock screen for easy access.

There are several ways to quickly open the camera application, the first of which is from the lock screen. In the lock screen, there are usually three options below, and they're the *call option, unlock option and the camera option.* Users should note that the call option is only meant for emergency calls and you'll be able to make normal calls if the device is unlocked.

Once in the lock screen, you can swipe upwards from the camera option icon and it'll take you to the camera app immediately, with this you'd be able to take pictures and view them while your screen is still locked, although some of other camera features might be restricted in use till you unlock your device.

Another quick way to open the camera application is by unlocking your device and navigating to the camera application from the home screen, and tap on it. This way, you'll get all features of the camera application and you'd be able to view all previous and present pictures.

How to take a picture

In this section, our primary aim is to teach you how to take pictures with the camera application, all you need to do is follow the procedures given below;

1.   Navigate to the camera app and open it using any of the methods we've explained in the first section. *(NB: Users should note that the camera app can also be launched by double clicking the side key, also when launching the camera from the lock screen, be aware that some features might not be available to you.)*

2.   Focus the camera on a particular image; tap the center of the image so the camera would focus on it.

3.   After focusing the camera and you're satisfied with what you're seeing, simply tap the shutter button below to take the shot. The white circular button beneath the camera interface is the shutter button. *(See image below)*

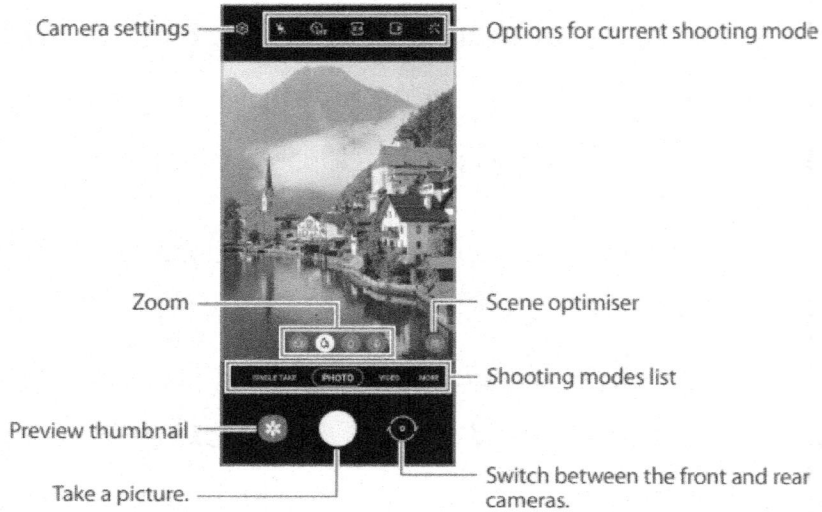

4.   Choose the shooting mode you prefer from the section above, also you zoom in, switch cameras and explore the camera settings. The image above shows it all for better understanding.

5.   The preview thumbnail can be used to view pictures that have been taken; however this varies depending on the shooting mode and camera being used.

6.   It is advisable to take images from a good distance in order not to zoom in or out because

zoomed pictures might not give you the quality you require.

7.   If you take a picture and it's blurry, use a clean cloth or tissue to dab the camera lens, then take the shot again.

8.   If any of the lenses are damaged, the camera may not work for some features.

9.   That's just a simple way to take a picture using the Samsung galaxy S21.

How to record a video

Recording a simple video on Samsung S21 is similar to taking a picture, users can record video easily just by tapping the video record shutter button. You can also switch between different video modes, choosing your preferred mode.

In this section, we would be teaching you how to take a simple video record using your new Samsung S21.

1.   Once in the camera app, swipe the shooting modes list to move to VIDEO or choose VIDEO from the list.

2.   Select the video recording shutter button to start recording a video.

3.   While recording a video, you might want to change in between the front and back cameras, swipe upwards or downwards to switch to either front or rear camera. Also, you can tap the option to perform the switch function.

4.   Tap the shutter button again to stop recording the video.

5.   Zooming a video for a long period while recording might result in low-quality results. This is done not to cause overheating for your device. So it is advisable to reduce zooming while recording a video.

That's how to perform a simple video recording using your Samsung S21, in the coming chapters of this book; we'll talk more about videos.

CHAPTER TWO

Rear Camera capabilities

The rear camera ability of the Samsung S21 is the real deal of the device; it is one big reason why most users go for the Samsung S21. The incredible features and ability that the Samsung S21 camera possesses will be discussed extensively in this section.

First of all, the rear cameras of the Samsung S21 possess four (*Actually Three Main types*) different types of lenses with each performing different functions in a photograph. There's the Ultra wide lens, Wide lens, Telephoto lens 1, and Telephoto lens 2. Samsung S21+ and Ultra doesn't possess the Telephoto 2 lens camera at the rear, it is only available in the Samsung S21.

For specifications, the Samsung S21 ultra wide lens is 12Megapixels, F2.2, 120° spanning up to 13mm. The wide lens possesses 108Megaixels, F1.8, 83° spanning 24mm while the first telephoto lens possesses 10Megapixels, F2.4, 35° and spans up to 72mm. The last but not the least of which is the Telephoto 2 possesses the same 10Megapixels, F4.9, 10° and will span almost 240mm.

These specifications are what the Samsung S21 rear cameras are made of, which is why they're mostly needed by individuals for photography reasons.

Front Camera capabilities

In this section we should be looking at the front camera capabilities of the Samsung S21, individuals like taking crisp and clear HD selfies, which is why the Samsung S21 front selfie camera is just the best answer.

For specifications the front camera of the Samsung S21 possesses 40Megapixels which captures very beautiful and detailed selfies. In the coming chapters of this book, we'll talk more about the front camera and what it can do.

What is the Aperture mode?

As a photography lover, there are some terms that shouldn't be new to you, one of them is the Aperture Mode. In this section, we would be talking about the aperture mode, what it works for.

Firstly, what is Aperture? It can simply be defined as a narrow space in a lens in which light passes through into the camera. The aperture is expressed in numbers such as f2.2 f1.8 as we've shown in the rear camera specifications above. Adjusting the aperture means that you're increasing or decreasing the space in which light comes right into the lens of the camera, typically this is done by the camera lens. That's everything about the Aperture mode.

CHAPTER THREE

How to take burst photos

This section teaches you how to take burst photos easily on your Samsung galaxy S21, it's quite easy. If you don't know what burst photos are, here's the explanation below;

Burst photos are series of the different photos taken almost at once, trying it out would give you a practical example of what burst mode really is. Burst photos is mostly used when capturing moving items, it gives you the opportunity to choose from many similar photos. Now that you've gotten the idea of what burst mode is, now go below and practice it using your new Samsung galaxy S21.

1.   Open the camera application from the home screen of your Samsung S21.

2.   On the top right corner of the camera interface, you'll see something like a setting icon, click on it and it'll open up a list of options.

3.   Select the option which says *swipe shutter button to* and then choose **take burst photos.**

4.   Now go back to your camera interface and swipe the shutter button downwards, immediately your device will start taking a series of shots, the counts will be displayed on the shutter button so you know when to stop.

5.   Now you can go to your gallery and choose a photo of your choice from the series you've taken.

6.   That's how to take a burst photo.

How to use optimal image stabilization

Optical image Stabilization or OIS is a feature available on both the Samsung galaxy S20 and S21 device. This feature makes both software and hardware processes that typically allow you to take very clear and detailed photos in any environment even if there isn't enough light. Because of the multi Camera rear camera that the Samsung galaxy S21 possesses, the camera system has dual OIS which is used for steady capturing and this doesn't matter if you're using the wide or telephoto lenses.

The OIS makes you take photos anytime of the day and still get the correct clear and detailed image you need.

If you wish to activate the video stabilization of your Samsung S21 device, try using the procedures below;

1.   Launch the camera application from the home screen of your Samsung Galaxy S21.

2.   Click on the settings icon at the top right corner of the device

3.   Swipe downwards and activate video stabilization, if you activated it already and want to deactivate it, toggle the switch.

4.   After this, go back to the camera interface and continue your video session.

5.   Doing this will allow the video to be more stable than usual.

How to choose the best external device for your Galaxy S21

Samsung S21 no longer makes use of Micro SD as they ditched the idea in 2020, so if you'd be thinking that the Samsung S21 may possess Micro SD slot, you're totally wrong. There's no Micro SD slot, and that's why we've decided to write this section in this guide is to show you some of the best alternative external devices you can use for your Samsung S21 device.

Here are some nice external devices we've listed below:

1.   **Samsung T7 500GB portable SD:** This is the first and most popular external device that can be recommended for your new Samsung S21 device. It is covered in an incredible design that can stand many dangerous effects. The external device comes with USB-C cables right inside the box upon purchase.

Because of the durable design and very fast transfers from your Samsung S21, that is why we recommend it as the first and best alternative external devices. The Samsung T7 500GB portable SD can be gotten for $90 only on Amazon, price may vary on other online stores.

2.   **Anker SD card reader:** if you possess a Micro SD card previously and you and some important data inside the SD card, then you'd need an external card reader to access those files. The Anker SD card reader is one of the top picks card readers for the

job. Durable and portable, the Anker SD card reader possesses slots for both Micro SD and normal SD cards. The Anker SD card reader can be gotten for $13 only on Amazon; price may vary on other online stores.

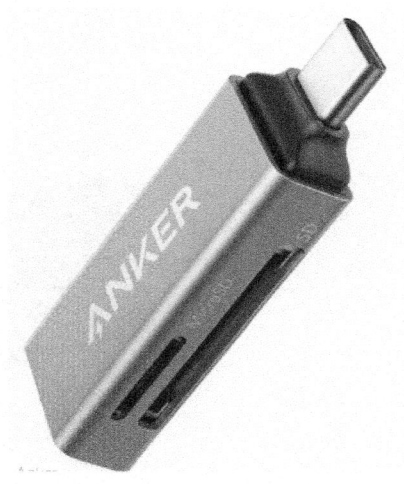

3.   Samsung Duo Plus 256 GB USB-C USB 3.1 flash drive: This amazing flash drive gives you the ease of access to the files saved on your drive. With this device, you'll be able to transfer photos and videos right from your device into the flash drive using a USB-C cable. It's a good backup for your photos and videos, the Samsung Duo plus cost only $45 on Amazon, value on other online stores may vary.

These three external devices are the most valued and popular external device, which you could use to back up your Samsung galaxy S21. Individuals are advised to choose according to their financial abilities.

CHAPTER FOUR

How to use portrait mode

The portrait mode is an incredible feature which is available in new versions of android devices, this fecture is also available in the Samsung galaxy S21 and it's more efficient and amazing. In this section, we would be teaching you everything you need to know about portrait mode and how you can make use of it, thereby improving your photography skills.

The portrait mode is a simple image that blurs the background of a subject when captured, giving the main subject a sharp and highly detailed look. The background blurriness gives the photo a kind of soft feeling and makes it look cooler than normal snapshots.

Now that you know what portrait mode is, the steps below will teach you how to take images using the portrait mode;

1.   Open the camera application from the home screen of your Samsung galaxy S21

2.   On the camera interface, swipe till you find MORE

3.   Select Portrait from the option

4.   Choose any of the portrait effects that's available.

5.   Also select a background effect that you'd like

6.   Background intensity can also be adjusted to your preferred way, this means you might not want the background entirely blur or too blurry,

7.   After all adjustments, select the shutter button to take the photo, hold still till your photo appears in the thumbnail.

8.   That's it, you just took a shot using portrait mode!

How to use night mode

Night mode is another popular feature that is also available in many other devices as well as the Samsung galaxy S21. The feature is one of a kind, because it allows you to take clear and crisp pictures in an environment with low light.

To capture a photo using the night mode feature, we've shown steps below;

1.   Open the camera application from the home screen of your Samsung galaxy S21

2.   On the camera interface, swipe till you find MORE

3.   Select Night mode from the option, the icon is a crescent moon.

4.   Focus the camera on the subject you wish to capture.

5. Afterwards, hold down the shutter button, and you'll see that the crescent moon will start turning into a full moon.

6. Once it turns into a complete full moon, your shot has been taken, and you'll see the brightness in a low light environment.

7. That's it, simple right? You just took a shot using night mode.

About scene Optimizer

This is another common term that you need to know as a photographer, the scene optimizer, although first introduced in the old Samsung S9 device is now available across many Samsung devices which include the Samsung galaxy S21. Scene optimizer is a feature that is placed in the Samsung Ai camera which helps it to detect subjects automatically without you having to focus on it; also it adjusts beautifully, helping you take cool images. The scene optimizer modifies the exposure, white balance and contrast of an environment, it also chooses modes.

Some of the modes it chooses includes; vehicles, drinks, Face, baby, person, dog, cat, food, sunrise, city, snow, rain, waterfall, sky, text, greenery, mountain, sunset, and many others.

To use the scene optimizer on your Samsung galaxy S21, please use the following procedures below;

1.   Open the camera application from the home screen of your Samsung galaxy S21

2.   Scene optimizer is available on the camera app by default, so there's no worry about activation.

3.   Hold till the camera detects a subject, and then tap the shutter button to take the shot.

4.   That's it; you just took a photo that was scene optimized.

CHAPTER FIVE

How to activate focus enhancer

If you wish to get a better focus when capturing photos using your Samsung galaxy S21, then you should activate the focus enhancer feature. This feature allows you to get better focus on subjects and objects while capturing, thereby producing detailed and well captured images.

To enable the focus enhancer, follow the steps shown below;

1.   Open the camera application from the home screen of your Samsung galaxy S21

2.   Select Photo Mode

3.   Tap the screen to reveal hidden options on the panels

4.   There's a white double circled icon on the bottom left of your device

5.   Select that icon to activate focus enhancer, see image below for better explanation.

6.   After focusing, select the shutter button to capture an image and hold still till it's shown in the thumbnail.

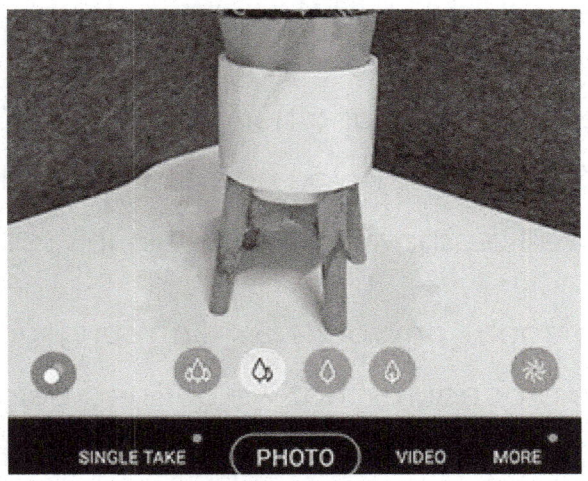

7.   That's it; you just captured a photo after using the focus enhancer!

Zooming

The rear camera lenses contribute to the zooming ability of the Samsung galaxy S21, as we discussed earlier, there are approximately four lenses on the rear of the Samsung S21 device, there's the standard zoom, followed by an ultra-wide lens, 3x optical zoom and 10x optical zoom respectively. With all these lenses, you can perform a 30x zoom on your Samsung galaxy S21; the next section will be teaching you how to use the space zoom feature.

How to use space zoom

Space zooming is just another name for the 30x zoom, with the Samsung S21, you can zoom a picture up to 30x and we'll be showing you that in this section.

To space zoom on your new Samsung galaxy S21, follow the procedures that we outlined below;

1.   Open the camera application from the home screen of your Samsung galaxy S21

2.   On the screen tap the zoom feature, it's a number on the screen, or just pinch the screen and spread your hands.

3.   You'll see ratio of your zoom below as you zoom, see the picture below;

4. Drag the slider till you hit the 30x zoom.

5. The image below shows 3x zoom

6. The image below shows 10x zoom

7. The image below shows 30x zoom

How to use live focus

The live focus is only available in video mode in the Samsung S21, on the note20; you'd see a live focus for images. In this section, we'll be teaching you everything about live focus and how you can use it.

The live focus video is almost the same with the portrait video, because they make use of the same options, using the live focus mode, it adds an effect to any video you're recording. Now to use the live focus feature, follow the steps we've outlined below;

1.   Open the camera application from the home screen of your Samsung galaxy S21

2.   Once on the camera interface, swipe to the right till you find MORE, select it and a panel of list will drop down.

3.   Choose Live Focus Video.

4.   There's a circle in the bottom right corner of the viewfinder, tapping the circle reveals four options which are; Blur, Glitch, Color point and Big circle.

29

5. Choose any one you like and tap the shutter button to begin recording. See image below.

How to use super slow-mo

As a photography freak, you'd know how to record a video using slow-mo; however, there's a better option, which is the super slow-mo. In this section, we would be showing you how to perform a super slow-mo recording.

To record videos using the super slow-mo feature, use the steps below;

1.   Open the camera application from the home screen of your Samsung galaxy S21

2.   Once on the camera interface, swipe to the right till you find MORE, select it and a panel of list will drop down

3.   Choose super slow-mo

4.   Select either Automatic or Manual

5.   Automatic mode records as soon as movements is detected within the square

6.   Manual mode will record as soon as you press the shutter button

7.   If you chose automatic, focus the camera on the subject and await a movement

8.   If you choose manual, once the camera is focused, and the subject has begun its movement, select the shutter button.

9.   Tap the shutter button again to stop the record.

10. That's the simple way of recording a super slow-mo video on Samsung S21.

CHAPTER SIX

How to add effects while on video call

During a video call, Samsung users can use different effects, which the other caller can see regardless of whatever phone they're using. However, this depends on the application and also depends on the device too. If you wish to use the video call effects while performing a video call, you'll need to activate the feature first. In this section, we would be showing you how to use effects during a video call.

To use video calling effects, follow the steps that we've carefully outlined below;

1.   Launch the settings application on your Samsung galaxy S21 home screen

2.   Swipe downwards till you see ADVANCED FEATURES

3.   Select it.

4.   Go down the list of options till you get to the bottom

5.   Select VIDEO CALL EFFECTS

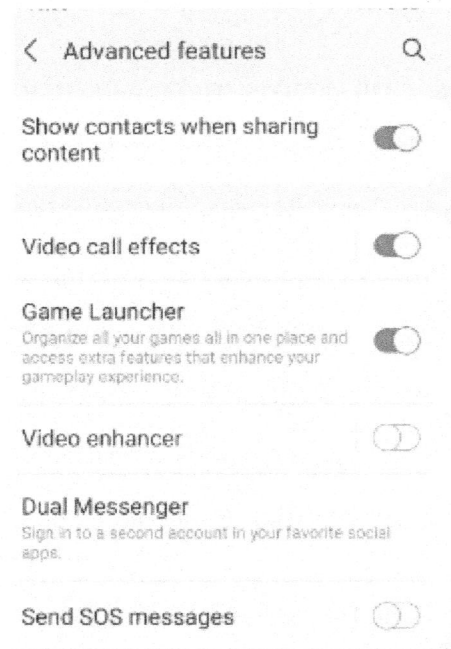

6.   If the effects toggle is deactivated, activate by toggling the switch again

7.   Choose the Background effect you wish to use.

After performing every step we listed above, you can now use video calling effects when you're performing a video call. Although it depends on the application, as for now, the video call effects works for Google Duo, Cisco WebEx, Zoom and Microsoft Teams.

Now, if you have any of the apps listed above, you can try out making video calls with it, you'll see an iccn at the top corner of the device, select it and you'd be able to choose the effect you want.

Also, it is important to note that the video calling feature was first introduced in the Samsung S21 series and is not available in previous Samsung devices.

How to activate show palm

For a photographer lover, you might have heard about Show palm; however, if you haven't heard about Show palm, we'll be showing you everything about Show palm in this section.

Firstly, what's Show Palm? Show palm is an easy way to take selfies without having to tap the shutter button allowing you to make a perfect posture and taking shots without having to stress pressing the shutter button. The Show palm is mostly used for selfies, although it may seem embarrassing to do in public.

Now that you know what Show palm is, let's show you how to activate the Show palm and also how to make use of it.

To activate Show palm, follow the instructions we've outlined below;

1.   Launch the camera application from your Samsung galaxy S21 home screen

2.   Select the settings icon at the top right corner of the camera interface.

3.   Go down the list till you find the **Front camera** settings

4.   Toggle the switch next to the Show palm option

Doing the above activates Show palm, now the below steps will guide you on how to use Show palm.

1.   Launch the camera application from your Samsung galaxy S21 home screen

2.   Tap the switch button to change over to the front selfie camera

3.   Place the camera in front of you, if there are friends behind you, let them appear to.

4.   Now showcase the palm of your hand in front of the selfie camera *(NB: Your other hand)*

5.   A yellow square like stuff will suddenly appear on your hand, when this happens, it means that the camera has detected your palm.

6.   A two seconds timer would be quickly initiated and a selfie would be taken.

7.   The rule is, make sure you remove your hand from the front camera once the timer is activated.

Activating 8K video

Recording videos in 8k is the best because it'd bring out the quality and HD crisp video that you require. Maybe you bought your Samsung S21 for filming or video recording purposes, the 8K video would be a very unique feature to you. In this section, we'll be showing you how to activate and record videos using 8K.

In other to activate and start recording your videos in 8K, follow the steps that we've carefully outlined below;

1.   Launch the camera application from the Samsung galaxy S21 home screen

2.   Select VIDEO to switch to video mode in the camera interface.

3.   You'll see an icon located at the top right corner of the video mode interface, it's the resolution icon, select it and set the resolution to 8k which is 24 frames per second.

4.   When your subject is ready to be filmed, select the shutter button to begin the record.

5.   Tap the shutter button again to end the video when you're done. Videos recorded will be saved in your gallery.

However, users should note that 8K videos use up a lot of space on the Samsung device, and the S21 series being a device that doesn't make use of Micro SD card; you might not enjoy it very well unless you get a perfect external storage device.

In the next chapter, we would show you how to add background music to your videos and some other features.

CHAPTER SEVEN

How to apply background music to video clip

Did you record a great film while using the incredible 8K feature? And you wish to add music to it? Then this section is for you, in this section we would be teaching you how to add background music to your videos.

The great thing about adding background music to your videos is that, on Samsung galaxy S21, you don't need to download any application as the inbuilt Samsung video editor is perfect for the job.

To add background music to your video, use the steps we've outlined below;

1.   Launch the gallery application from your Samsung S21 home screen

2.   Select the video that you wish to add background music to

3.   Choose EDIT YOURSELF

4.   Select the pencil icon, which is located in the left corner beneath the screen, after you choose that, you'll be taken to the Samsung video editor.

5.   Now you'll be able to add background music and do a lot of other stuff on your Samsung video editor, it's very easy.

How to join multiple video clips to make a video

Combining or joining multiple video clips to make a video can be easily done using almost the same process as the one above, this is because you're going to be using the same internal Samsung video editor. In this section, we would show you briefly how to join or combine multiple video clips to make one whole video.

The below steps will guide you through in combining videos and making a whole video out of it:

1.   Open the gallery application from the home screen of your Samsung galaxy S21

2.   Choose one of the videos which is part of the clip you want to combine

3.   Choose the edit icon at the bottom left corner of the screen, looking like a pencil.

4.   Choose Add, it is located at the top of the video editor interface

5.   Select all the videos you want to combine with the first one

6.   Images can also be picked too.

7.   Select done when you've finished choosing

8.   The video timeline will display at the bottom of the screen.

9.   Select save, located at the top of the video editor interface to complete your combined video.

CHAPTER EIGHT

Backup

Backup simply means backing up your device, this is a very good thing to do as no one can predict the future, which means no one will know the absolute time that their device would get spoiled or damaged which can lead to loss of data and files if not properly backed up.

Backing up files can be done in several ways which include backing up with external devices, backing up with one drive and backing up with Google cloud storage, anyone you wish to back up with is perfect, but in this guide, we're only allowed to give you procedures on how to backup with One Drive.

However, we can give you a brief explanation on backing up with external devices, to back up your Samsung S21 with your external device; you need to continue sending any files and data into the external devices either on a weekly basis or daily basis. So all files on your Samsung S21 will be duplicated in the external device.

How to backup videos and photos to onedrive account

This section is a very straightforward one; we'll be showing you how you can back up your device using the inbuilt OneDrive cloud storage, the OneDrive cloud storage gives you 30GB of free storage space for you to store your important files and data. Some of the things you can backup includes videos, documents, music and pictures. After backing up, you can easily access backed up files from a PC anywhere in the world, all you'd need to do is visit onedrive.live.com. Also, updating your settings to automatic backup can keep you safe from losing files as your device would be backed up automatically any time it is connected to the internet.

Here's how to back up files with OneDrive below;

1.   Slide up to reveal the app menu screen on your Samsung galaxy S21.

2.   Go to Microsoft Apps folder, and choose OneDrive.

3.   If you have a OneDrive account before, just select Sign in and fill in your email and password, but if you do not possess a OneDrive account, simply tap Sign up to create one instantly.

4.   Select the upload option, and then choose any document or files you wish to back up.

5.   You should be aware that backing up your device will cost you a lot of data subscriptions.

Also, you can sync your gallery with OneDrive to help you backup your photos easily, syncing your gallery with OneDrive, you'd be able to access the photos from any other device. Here's how to sync your gallery with OneDrive;

1.   Launch the gallery app from your Samsung galaxy S21 app menu

2.   Choose Menu, it's the three horizontal lines at the bottom.

3.   Select settings; now activate the option next to **sync with OneDrive.**

4.   Now your entire gallery has been synced with OneDrive, you can easily access them on the OneDrive Website.

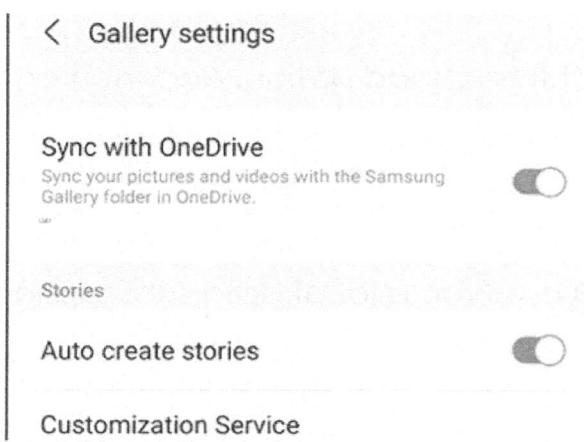

How to resize your image

You might want to use specific images for some reasons and you need to resize them to fit in to the requirements, don't worry! Resizing images just got easier with your Samsung galaxy S21. In this section, we would be showing the simple steps on how to resize your image.

To resize your image follow the detailed steps below;

1.   Launch the gallery application from your Samsung galaxy S21 app screen

2.   Choose any image you wish to resize.

3.   Select the pencil icon which stands for editing

4.   You'll see three dots on the top right corner of the editing interface, select it.

5.   Choose **resize** on the list that comes up.

6.   Modify to your preferred resized percentage then select done to authenticate changes.

7.   After resizing your photo, you'll see in the image details that the size was reduced to your preferred percentage.

That's all; if you performed the steps above, you've successfully resize an image, now you can try it on other images that you wish to resize.

CHAPTER NINE

How to convert HEIF photo to JPEG

HEIC photo format cannot be viewed or used on Androids unless you convert them to JPEG, although, Apple has now allowed their devices to support HIEC photo format but Androids which Samsung is included haven't thought about the idea yet, which means you still have to convert your HEIC photo format to JPEG if you want to make use of it on the Samsung galaxy S21.

In this section, we would be showing you how to convert the HIEC photo format to JPEG, it's simple and easy, all you have to do is follow the procedures carefully.

Samsung doesn't have any image conversion tool or application that can convert HIEC photos to JPEG, so we ll be showing you some third party apps that can help you convert HIEC photo formats to JPEG. We'll be showing you one application and one website, so you can pick anyone you require.

Because there are many third party apps that can convert HIEC to JPEG we have chosen the best and most popular app for you, which is called LUMA. If you have a HIEC photo format and you want to convert to JPEG, you should download LUMA on your Samsung galaxy S21. Follow the procedures below to complete the conversion.

1.   Launch playstore from the home screen of your Samsung Galaxy S21.

2.   Search for LUMA and complete the download, afterwards install the LUMA app.

3.   The LUMA app is free from ads and is storage friendly.

4.   Launch the LUMA app and wait for it to load

5.   You'll see a screen with different options below, choose FROM HIEC since you're converting HIEC images to JPEG

6.   Select the addition + like icon, once you do that, two options will be presented to you, which are *Open single image and Open images folder.*

7.   The Open single image option allows you to select images one by one for the conversion why the Open images folder allows you to open any folder that possesses multiple HIEC images.

8.   Selecting Open single image, you can simply choose the image you want to convert individually, after choosing, simple select SAVE AS JPEG

9.   In the blink of an eye LUMA converts the image to JPEG, it's important to note that specifying where the images are saved are necessary, so you'd know where your new JPEG files are located.

10. If you have a folder filled with HIEC images and you want to convert all, simply select the Open image folder, and choose the folder, select images you wish to convert, then select CONVERT.

Now that you know how to use the LUMA app to convert HIEC images to JPEG, it's normal for us to give you another alternative in case you don't like using apps.

HIECTOJPEG is the best website you can use if you don't prefer using applications, the website is straightforward, we don't need to explain the procedures in steps for you to get it. Just visit HIECtoJPEG and upload your HIEC image and process them, download them once you're done. Easy as pie.

How to customize selfie color tone

After taking selfies, you may not like the color tone that's displaying, don't worry it's changeable. Changing the selfie color tone helps you modify images to your taste and preference. For those that prefer warm color tones on their selfies, Samsung has a feature for you. In this section, we would be teaching you how to customize and modify your selfie tone.

This hidden Samsung trick allows you to choose from different color tones saving you the stress of going through photo editing apps searching for filters and effects so you can change the color balance and temperature. Samsung color tones give you the warm and natural look that your image deserves. Changing the color tone doesn't take much of a step.

Here's how to perform the function below:

1.   Launch the camera application from your Samsung galaxy S21 home screen

2.   Switch your camera to selfie mode

3.   Select the setting icon which is located at the top left corner of the camera interface

4.   Go downwards till you see the Selfie color tone option

5.   Choose it, and then select your preferred color tone.

How to activate tracking autofocus

First of all, what is Autofocus? Auto focus is a feature that allows you to focus or lock a subject when taking snapshots, when it is locked; you get sharper and clearer images. The autofocus tracking works for situations whereby the object or subject is moving such as during sports, children and pets. In this section, we would be showing you how to activate the tracking Autofocus.

Use the steps available below to activate the feature above:

1.   Launch the camera app on your Samsung galaxy S21 home screen

2.   Go to photo mode

3.   Select any area on the screen, and then choose the lock icon to enable Autofocus. After activation, you'll be able to adjust and modify the light exposure around the shot by sliding and moving the bar until you get your preferred taste.

4.   After modification and focusing, select the shutter button to capture the shot.

5.   When the photo is captured, it'll appear in the thumbnail, tap it to view.

6.   That's for autofocus, now to activate tracking autofocus so you can capture moving objects easily, select the settings icon which is located at the top left corner of the camera's interface.

7.   Go downwards till you see tracking Autofocus, activate it.

8.   Now go back to the camera app and try capturing your unstable Toddler, moving objects or pets, they'll be kept in focus no matter how unstable they are.

CHAPTER TEN

How to activate voice command

Samsung has come up with another incredible feature which is available in the camera application, as a photography lover, this feature is one of the best for you. The Samsung galaxy S21 was specifically built to suit the needs of photography and videography that individuals want. Which is why in this guide, we would be showing every feature that concerns the camera app.

Because of the incredible and mouth watering features that Samsung has added to their camera application, even beginner photographers can take pictures that look like what should have been taken by a professional.

The voice command feature of the camera application is actually available in other devices, but if you're not familiar with android devices then you might get stuck in trying to activate it. That's why we've added it to this guide. In this section, we would be showing you how you can activate the voice command.

Following the procedures below, you'll find out how to take selfies just by using voice commands;

1.   Launch the camera application from your Samsung galaxy S21 home screen.

2.   Select the settings icon, which is located at the top left corner of the camera screen.

3.   Once in the settings screen, go downwards till you see **shooting modes**

4.   In the next screen, you'll see a list of shooting modes displayed for you, some of which are; show palm, floating shutter button, press volume keys and voice commands.

5.   Toggle the voice command switch to enable the voice command feature.

6.   After activating the feature, go back to your camera interface and use the voice commands to take pictures, you can use; "shoot", "cheese", "smile" and "capture" if you also wish to record a video using voice command just say "record video".

7.   This makes taking selfies and rear photo images with your friends easier and more fun.

In previous chapters of this book, we've shown you how to use the show palm feature too, that's another feature you can try out with your friends. To deactivate the voice command feature, use the same steps above and toggle the voice command switch again. However, we think most photography lovers will love using the command feature as it is stress free and would help you take pictures without the need of a tripod.

How to save photos and videos in high efficient

In this era smartphones does not only satisfy your multitasking needs such as watching videos, browsing the internet and maybe reading an eBook at the same time, there are hundreds of things that your smartphone can now perform, all what we've been talking about in this guide, I'm sure you never knew your device can actually do it, except for a few common ones. In this guide, we'll be showing you how you can save up photos and videos in high efficiency.

Saving images and videos in HEIF format is pretty easy, you just have to set it up in settings, the procedures below will take you through;

1.   Launch the settings application from your Samsung galaxy S21 home screen

2.   Choose **Format and Advanced options**

3.   Activate the switch of HEIF pictures

4.   Go over to Video mode and choose **Advanced recording**

5.   Enable the High efficiency video switch

6.   That's all, very simple and straightforward.

Doing this, Samsung galaxy S21 will now save video and photos in HEIF formats and won't compromise any detail or quality when saving. HIEF formats are smaller than the regular JPEG formats.

You can also convert the HEIF formats back to JPEG if need be, just head to Google and look for the best site that converts HEIF images to JPEG.

Activating HDR+10 shooting

HDR+ 10 which full meaning is High Dynamic range + 10 is a feature that gives your photos and videos standard reproduction of color. It is a feature built specifically to enhance color range as well as dynamic brightness. In this section, we'll be showing you how to use the HDR+ 10 feature to shoot videos with a wide range of colors and depth, bringing out your videos and photos more vivid and true to life.

It is therefore important to note that the HDR+10 feature is not available when video is being recorded at 60 frames per second. The HDR+10 feature will not work unless you activate it in the camera settings, some Samsung devices do not possess the HDR+10 feature, so that's an addition to you for getting the Samsung galaxy S21.

Below are the steps you should follow to activate the HDR+10 feature;

1.   Launch the camera application from the home screen of your Samsung galaxy, S21.

2.   Select the settings icon; it's located at the top left corner of the camera interface.

3.   Select REAR VIDEO SIZE, and then tap 16:9, also set the resolution to FHD 1920 X 1080. It is important to note that HDR+10 will only work with that video resolution.

4. Go back, and then select **Advanced recording options** in the camera settings.

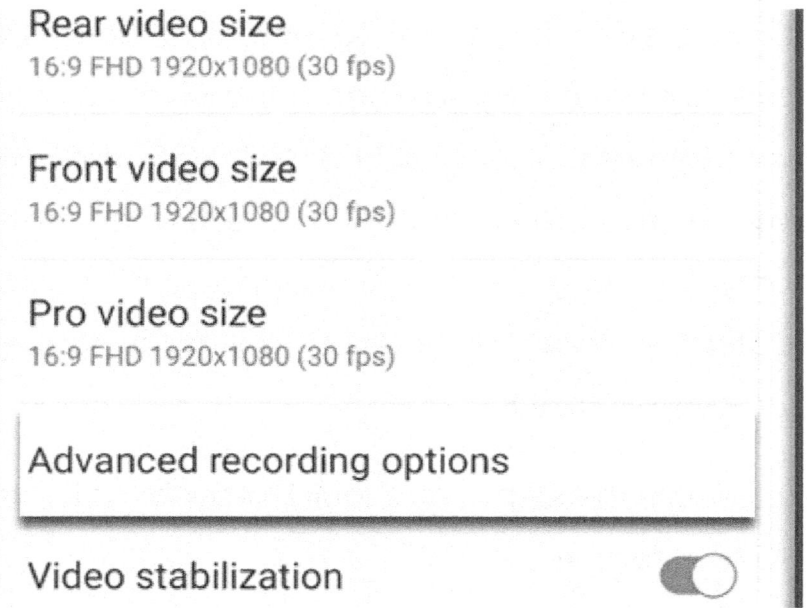

5. Select the HDR+10 switch.

6. That's all; you can now take your videos in HDR+10.

CHAPTER ELEVEN

Extracting high-resolution image from a video

After taking a video in 8k, you can still take a screenshot image from that video, this is known as extracting a high-resolution image from a video and that's what we would be teaching you in this section.

Extracting high-resolution images from a video is pretty easy and doesn't take a whole lot of process.

Here's how to do it below;

1.   Launch the gallery application from the app screen of your Samsung S21

2.   Select or pick any 8K video that you've recorded.

3.   Choose or tap the capture button, it's located at the top left corner of the screen.

4.   This takes the shot, you can also take more shots from the video footage, as much as you like.

5.   All screenshots or captures are 33 megapixels images.

How to shoot 12-bit RAW

The 12-bit RAW is only available on the Samsung S21 ultra; so if you're a user of the Samsung galaxy S21 or S21+ you won't be able to use this feature. For individuals who use the Samsung S21 ultra. 12-bit RAW is a new incredible feature that Samsung added to the ultra in order to boost its camera ability and features.

According to our research, RAW files are actually "digital negatives", what this means is that they do not record digital sharpness or white balance in an image, and this makes the image much more basic and good for photo editing. The 12-bit RAW feature is made for professional photographers, so if you're a professional photographer reading this guide, you should find the 12-bit RAW easy to use.

However, whether professional or not, the 12-bit RAW can be used by anybody as far as you're using the Samsung galaxy S21 ultra and you're following this guide. 12-bit RAW is said to capture more dynamic range which results in well detailed and highlighted images. It's a professional feature, that's why before you can shoot in 12-bit RAW, you have to go to MORE and activate PRO MODE. In PRO MODE, you'll see several settings and this is where your photography skills come in, experiment will be a good start.

Although before you can shoot in RAW mode, you need to activate it in the camera settings, head to the camera settings, select FORMAT AND ADVANCED OPTIONS, then activate RAW copies; this allows your device to take a RAW image and a JPEG image as well.

It is therefore important to note that the raw copies or files take up more space than regular JPEG images, so the feature should be turned off when not in use, unless you like it that way.

Shooting single take 2.0

Single Take, this is another incredible feature that Samsung has made available for its users. The single take feature allows you to capture the best moments, you can use single take to capture wide-angle shots, close-up shots as well as videos.

One amazing thing about the single take feature is that fine tuning the recording time is absolutely doable. In this section, we would be showing you how to take shots using a single take.

Following the steps below, you'll be able to take single take shots;

1.   Launch the gallery application from the app screen of your Samsung S21

2.   Select Single Take from the options menu

3.   Select the shutter button, and then pan the device around to capture best shots and scene clips. Camera automatically captures best shots and clips.

4.   When done, select the thumbnail, you'll find all the images you've taken there.

5.   If you want to view the results, move the icon upwards

6.   To save results individually, choose select then tick the ones you wish to save.

7.   Afterwards, select the arrow icon that's facing downwards.

The single takes AI, captures up to ten different kinds of images and four different kinds of videos, and all these are captured from 3-10 seconds.

All the single take results are saved in the gallery.

CHAPTER TWELVE

How to reset camera app settings

There are sometimes when you'd have tweaked the camera app settings, and it's now feels like trash, too much of modification can make your camera settings stupid and you'll want to reset it to its default settings. That's absolutely what we'll be showing you in this section, using the process below, you should be able to reset your camera settings in no time.

1.   Launch the camera application from the home screen of your Samsung S21

2.   Choose settings, it is located at the top left corner of the camera interface

3.   Select GENERAL

4.   Choose RESET then choose YES

Very short procedure, if you perform the above function, you've successfully reset your camera app settings.

How to use Bokeh

Adding the Bokeh effect to your photos is a good way to use depth of field, the bokeh feature is quite different from the portrait feature. In this section, we'll be showing you how to add Bokeh to your pictures. We've listed the steps required below;

1.   Launch the camera application from the home screen of your Samsung S21

2.   Switch to the rear camera of the device.

3.   Swipe till it gets to Live focus mode

4.   Make sure light comes through from the background before you take a photo

5.   Check the image taken and modify the blurred background

6.   Modify and adjust options then select "tick" to save the photo.

That's all; you've successfully added Bokeh to your picture.

CHAPTER THIRTEEN

How to zoom in and zoom out

This is a basic function and as a photographer you really shouldn't be taught this; however, for some reasons we decided to add this guide in order to make it a complete and well comprehensive guide for beginners as well as professional photographers. In this section, we'll be showing you how to zoom in and zoom out.

Here are the easy steps below:

1. Launch the camera application from the home screen of your Samsung S21

2. To zoom in, pinch the camera interface with your two fingers.

3. Spread the two pinched fingers to zoom out

4.   You can also drag the slider to the left or right to zoom in or out.

How to configure shooting mode

There are different shooting modes in the new Samsung galaxy S21 and as an expert or beginner photography it is advisable that you try out all the modes and master them so as to render them effectively when shooting on a paid service.

How do you arrange or configure shooting modes isn't actually necessary, what's important is trying out these modes.

Here are some incredible shooting modes that are available in the Samsung S21;

1.   **Singe Take:** We've discussed this shooting mode in previous chapters of this book

2.   **HDR+10 mode:** We've also discussed this mode, explaining extensively how it works.

3.   **108MP mode:** This mode is only available for users of the Samsung S21 ultra, if you're using the Samsung S21 or S21+, then you won't be able to use this mode. Activating the 108MP mode isn't difficult at all, in the camera app, just select the 3:4 108MP and that's all, you've enabled 108MP mode and can now take shots with it.

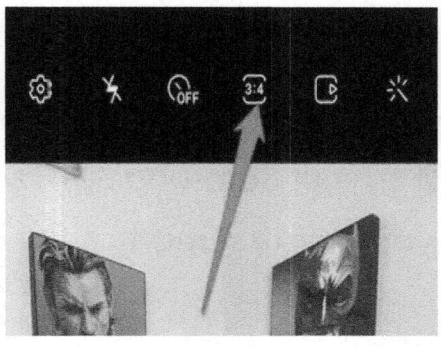 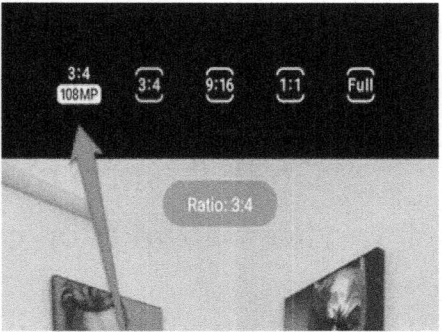

4.   **Directors View mode:** We'll be showing you how to use this mode and more about it in the coming chapters of this book.

5.   **Panoramas Mode:** This mode is easily accessible; you'll find it in more items.

There are other modes that aren't mentioned above; however, it is important you try out all the modes available in your device.

AR Zone features

AR zone features is what we'd be discussing in this section, AR zone is filled with different AR emojis and AR doodles, In this zone you can select any of the features you prefer and capture fun videos and photos.

Here's how to get to the AR zone features;

1.   Go to the app menu of your Samsung S21 by sliding from down to up on your home screen

2.   Choose the Samsung folder

3.   Select AR zone.

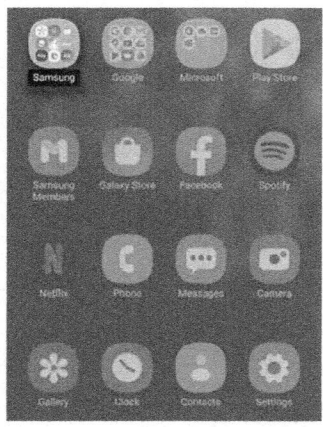

4.   Once in the AR zone application, you'll be able to access all the AR features.

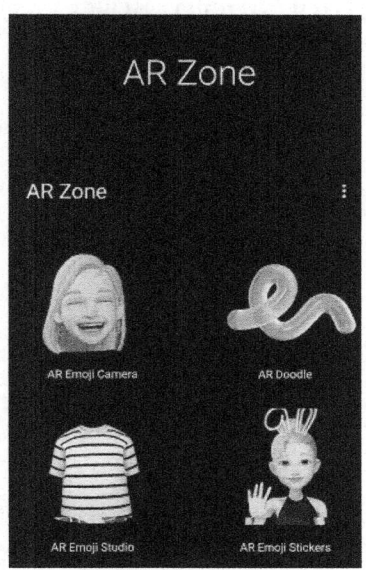

5.   Some of the AR features include;

- **Quick Measure:** Size and distance of the object or subject can be measured hastily.
- **AR Doodle:** This allows you to record videos making them fun by using visual handwritings, drawings on faces and so on.
- **AR Emoji camera:** Build an emoji that looks just like you; you can also take pictures or record videos using My emoji.

- **Deco pic:** Take snapshots and record videos with various stickers.
- **AR Emoji studio:** Build your own My emoji stickers.

CHAPTER FOURTEEN

Computational photography

This may sound new to you, but as a photographer, computational photography is one of the terminologies you should know. In this section, we would be explaining briefly what computational photography is.

What is computational photography?

Computer photography can simply be defined as the use of computer processing abilities in different cameras to manufacture an improved image which will go beyond what the lens and sensor takes up in a single shot.

This computational photography is now available in most smartphones and Samsung galaxy S21 is one of those smartphones that possess enhanced computational photography. Computational photography improves images using different methods and processes, adding depth of field, reducing motion blur and enhancing color and brightness is what computational photography does.

As the level of photography improves drastically in smartphones, computational photography is now one of the most searched keywords online, as every photographer wants to know what computational photography is. In this section, I guess we've shown you and given you insight on what computational photography is.

It is therefore important to note that computational photography brings out the uniqueness and quality of an image.

HP Sprocket

HP sprocket is an application which is available to android users, you can use HP sprocket to edit, print or share your photos.

You can download the HP sprocket app from Playstore and use it to edit your photos. To edit photos on the HP sprocket app, simply click on the pencil icon, you can apply filters; add frames, text, stickers and many more. You can also resize and rotate your image using your two fingers to pinch zoom.

Selecting the printer icon prints out your photo. Save photos, you've edited and also print, or share them to loved ones.

Use Photobooth on Hp sprocket; Photobooth allows you to take four photos in a row. After installing the Hp sprocket app, launch it and swipe to Photobooth, select the shutter button to take photobooth images, explore and see how it works.

HP sprocket seems like the best app to use for Photo ID. to use Hp Sprocket for photo ID, use the procedures below;

1.   Launch the Hp sprocket app.

2.   Follow the command for choosing backgrounds, getting rid of accessories and positioning your face or a friend's face.

3.   Select the photo dimensions.

There are other sections you can check out in the Hp sprocket app, sections like Custom stickers and Tile printing, these sections are straightforward and understandable.

Mpow Selfie Stick Tripod

The Mpow selfie stick Tripod is one of the best of its kind, as it has multiple uses, it's beautiful and stress free to use. In this section, we'll be discussing the features and usage of the Mpow selfie stick tripod. The Mpow tripod has adjustable light making your visual world more amazing and embellished. The upgraded tripod stand that the Mpow selfie stick possesses can serve multiple purposes such as; a mobile phone tripod, an action camera tripod and a desktop phone holder. This Tripod can be used with your Samsung galaxy S21, which is why we've included it in this guide.

CHAPTER FIFTEEN

How to use Trash bin

The trash bin is a place where deleted photos and files go to, on your Samsung device, when a file is deleted; it is transferred to the trash bin and kept there for 30 days before it is removed permanently. In this section, we would be showing you how you can restore photos or files that you've deleted but you want them back.

If you mistakenly deleted a file or photo from your Samsung device, do not fret, you can easily get it back just by going to the trash bin and restoring it; however, make sure to make up your mind before 30 days else it would be deleted permanently and there'd be no way to get it back.

There are two places that you can restore from, it's either you're restoring from the Gallery app or you're restoring from the My files app. Don't worry we'll show you how to go about using each of them.

If you mistakenly deleted photos, restoring them from the gallery app is faster, here's how to do it below;

1.   Launch the gallery app from your Samsung galaxy S21 app screen.

2.   To restore already deleted photos, select

3.   Choose **Recycle bin** from the list of options

4.   Choose the photo or video, that you'd like to restore

5.   Then choose , the image will be restored.

6.   To restore multiple images, tap and hold an image then select the others you wish to restore, then tcp on **Restore**

Now if you deleted a document, ringing tone or any file and you wish to restore it, using the "My files app" is the best way. See steps below;

1.   Launch the My files app from your Samsung galaxy S21 app screen.

1.   Select the three dots icon ⋮

2.   Choose recycle bin from the list of options

3.   Tap and hold the file you wish to restore.

4.   Choose restore.

Simple as that, you've successfully learnt how to restore images and files.

Using Galaxy S21 to snap images of the stars

The Samsung galaxy S21 and S21 ultra have been said to be a device that can turn individuals into astrophotographers. Taking pictures of the Milky Way is not an easy thing because you'd need a lot of equipment and photography skills to achieve that feat. However, in this guide, we've decided to bring up this topic in order to teach our readers the simplest way of taking images of the stars. As far as you've got your Samsung galaxy S21, S21+ or ultra, you're one step ahead.

With Samsung's drastic improvement in their camera features, shooting the stars has become the talk of the town as every photography freak wants to try it out, using the pro mode and some other photography skills, you should get a good shot of the milky way. Not to talk much, we'll be going straight to the steps on how to shoot images of the stars using your Samsung galaxy S21.

When going for a night capture, you should go when the moon isn't up, that is, a moonless night, this way you get a better view of the Milky Way. And you must take along with you a backup phone battery and also a rechargeable flashlight.

Follow the procedures below;

1.   On getting there, the first thing you should do is to set up your equipment.

2.   To shoot the stars, you need a tripod to help hold your device so as to avoid shaking, you'd also need

a remote shutter or timed shutter, because you'll need to make the camera very stagnant so it'd be ab e to absorb light.

3.   The Samsung camera isn't built for shooting the stars, so you'd have to do some settings to achieve this feat, use pro mode, you can find that in More items if you swipe down the different modes available on the camera app. Also make sure your camera is in mcnual mode not automatic, so you have control over everything.

4.   Modify and adjust shutter speed, use a slow shutter speed, because your shutter speed needs to be open for a little while in order for it to take in light for the capture. With this, you'd capture even star trails.

5.   Modify and adjust the white balance color, white balance reduces and increases the temperature of the camera, this means objects that seem white in your eye will actually display as white when the photo is ready. According to our research, 4500 or less would be suitable for astrophotography.

6.   Make your ISO sensitivity right; modify your ISO settings as it has a great impact on the image brightness, the higher the ISO the brighter your images. However, it isn't advisable to use too much ISO as it may affect and ruin the picture.

7.   We also discussed in this guide how to save files in RAW, so make sure you've switched to RAW before shooting the stars.

CHAPTER SIXTEEN

Ways to improve photography in Samsung Galaxy S21

All what we've taught you in this guide are actually the ways that you require in improving your Photography using the Samsung galaxy S21. However, we just intend to give you a brief on how you can up your photography game.

Arrange the modes at the bottom of your camera interface to the way you want it, this is very important and will make you look like a professional when taking photographs, we omitted this when we were discussing *How to configure shooting modes.* Arranging your shooting modes is one of the best ways to improve your photography as it gives you ease and less stress, so if you know the modes you use regularly or like best, you can arrange them one after the other on the bottom of your camera interface.

To arrange the shooting modes on your camera interface, here's what you need to do; select More on the end of the modes list. Then drag any mode in the More list into the bottom tray, to take away a mode you don't want, drag it to the tray, do this to edit and rearrange your shooting modes, then choose save when you're done.

After adjusting and rearranging your shooting modes, it'll be easy for you to capture beautiful moments with your Samsung S21.

Another way of improving your photography is by trying out new tips and tricks, trying out all the modes, tweaking stuff and exploring the camera application.

About director's view on GALAXY S21

The director's view is one of the shooting modes available in the Samsung galaxy S21, in the previous chapter of this guide; we told you that we'd be talking extensively on this subject. Now here we are, in this section, we'll discuss briefly about the director's view mode and how to activate it.

As the name implies the Director's view mode allows you to seamlessly use both the front and rear camera when recording a video, this mode makes you the director, you can work with both the rear and front camera simultaneously making your videos look like a directed film recording. Isn't that incredible? This mode is a very useful one for individuals who uses both cameras to record videos.

Activating the director's view mode is not something difficult, it's just a mode you pick from the shooting modes, here's how to activate it below;

1.   Launch your camera app from your Samsung galaxy S21 home screen.

2.   Choose more from the ribbon below, it may be written as More items.

3.   Select Director's view mode.

4.   Now start shooting that video.

CONCLUSION

In this guide we've talked about everything that can make you become a professional Samsung S21 photographer, after reading this guide completely, it'll be very easy for you to capture perfect and mind blowing images. Readers are advised to go through each section carefully to grasp the teachings and steps explained in them.

All the steps that we've outlined in this guide have been tested specifically so there's nothing wrong in any of the steps, if you don't understand a step, read it again for better assimilation. If you're a photography freak, you'll learn dozens of new things in this guide, and from a freak you'd become an export in mobile photography.

For users to understand and completely assimilate, we've decided to use simplest English with less grammar, anything you find hard to understand might be a term in photography which I'm sure we explained extensively in the guide. Each section tells you what you'll learn before you start reading, so you'd have an objective before you read a section.

Detailed images have been placed in specific places for more in-depth understanding of what the writer is trying to portray. This guide was prepared for Samsung S21 users who would love to know about how the Samsung S21 camera works, nevertheless, amateur and beginners mobile photographers would gain a lot from the guide.

ABOUT THE AUTHOR

Curtis Campbell is an intelligent and innovative computer scientist with experience in software engineering. As a renowned technology expert, his passion for capturing still photos and motion pictures has led him into photography and videography, which he is doing with excellence. Curtis has produced several tutorials on different topics. As a researcher and a prolific writer with proficiency in handling tech products, he learned different approaches to managing issues on the internet and other applications.

Made in the USA
Las Vegas, NV
15 September 2021